Meditations of a Tired Parent
Letters on Grace, Anger, and Showing Up Anyway

By
Phillip Deam
The Philosophical Dad

Dedication

For every parent who has whispered, "I can't do this anymore," and still did it anyway. This is for you.

Dear Reader

Parenting can be brutal, beautiful, exhausting, and sacred—all in the same breath.

This book isn't a manual. It's a series of letters from one tired parent to another. It's a companion for the days that feel long, the nights that feel longer, and the moments when you wonder if you're enough. Let me say this clearly: You are.

These reflections are here to walk with you—quietly, honestly, and without judgment.

How to Use This Book

Read one letter at a time. Let the words breathe. Reflect. Revisit them on the hard days. Each letter is paired with a thought to carry with you, and a question to help you ground the idea in your own experience. You don't have to race to the end. Just keep going. One moment at a time.

Letter 1: You're Not Failing—You're Just Tired
Letter 2: Meltdowns, Mornings, and Moments of Peace
Letter 3: The Power of Perspective
Letter 4: Presence Over Perfection
Letter 5: Anger, Guilt, and Emotional Control
Letter 6: This Is the Hardest Job You'll Ever Love
Letter 7: You're Doing Better Than You Think
Letter 8: The Weight of Comparison
Letter 9: Let Them Be Small
Letter 10: You Are The Anchor
Final Thoughts

Letter 1: You're Not Failing—You're Just Tired

They say Sisyphus was cursed by the gods—doomed to roll a boulder up a mountain, only for it to tumble back down, again and again, for all eternity.

Most hear that story and see punishment. But the philosopher Albert Camus saw something different. He imagined Sisyphus smiling. Not because the task was easy, but because he had accepted it as his own. Because the strength wasn't in finishing—it was in choosing to keep going.

And if that's not the definition of parenting, I don't know what is.

Because you, too, rise each day and face the same hill.
Same mornings. Same cries. Same reminders. Same mess.
You hold your child through storms you can't stop. You try to stay patient when your tank is empty. And sometimes—most of the time—it feels like no one notices.

But I see you.
Not from a distance, not from a pedestal, but from beside you. I've cursed at the sky in frustration. I've whispered apologies I didn't know how to make right. I've stared at the ceiling wondering if I'm

failing my children by being too tired to show up the way they need.

And here's what I've learned:

You're not failing. You're just tired.
 And tired doesn't mean weak. It means *you've been giving*—over and over and over.

There's a moment—almost every day—where I let out this long, exasperated sigh. A pause. A whisper of reflection where I wonder if I took the wrong path somewhere. Did I choose left at the fork when I should've gone right? It's not a regret, not exactly. Just weariness. I've spent the morning teaching my son—we homeschool, so I'm his full-time educator too. Every lesson is a careful balance of patience, encouragement, and trying to meet him where he is. Then I'm off to work for the rest of the day, only to pull into the driveway hours later and realize—I've missed my two youngest. Again. They're already asleep.

I sit there in the dark, engine off, lights out, forehead resting lightly against the headrest. Sometimes I just tap my head against the seat. Not hard. Just enough to say, *God, I'm tired.* Last night was another broken one—maybe four hours of sleep, and that was the fourth night in a row. I've heard people say, "God never gives us more than we can handle," but honestly? There are days where I feel like He's testing the hell out of that theory.

Today had one of those moments. I was trying to guide my son through a lesson, trying to keep the day on track, and he just wasn't having it. Total resistance. The noise from outside creeps in sometimes—people who think I should be firmer, stricter, more structured. They say he can't move forward unless he conforms. But I know him. I know that force won't work. I know when to push and when to pause. Still, the noise can be loud. Even when your heart knows the truth, doubt has a way of slipping through the cracks when you're tired enough.

But the moment passes. It always does. I step out of the car. My wife needs me now. There's no space for self-pity, no time to wallow. The day isn't over—not by a long shot. My son's still awake, and there's still work to do. So I gather myself, breathe deep, and push the stone again.

Reflective Thought:

There will be days when everything feels heavier than it should. When your fuse is short, your body aches, and your thoughts whisper lies about your worth. On those days, don't measure yourself by what didn't get done.

Measure yourself by the fact that you stayed.

You stayed, even tired. Even frayed. Even questioning everything.

And sometimes, that's what love looks like—it just looks like staying.

A Thought to Carry With You:

"The stone never gets lighter—but you get stronger." The Philosophical Dad

Reflective Question:

Where in your day do you feel the weight the most? And what does it mean to keep pushing through that moment, not perfectly—but purposefully?

Let it sit with you tonight. And tomorrow, when the hill appears again—know that you're not alone on the climb.

Letter 2: Meltdowns, Mornings, and Moments of Peace

They say Odysseus knew what was coming.

Before the Sirens sang—before their voices could twist his mind—he tied himself to the mast of his ship. He instructed his crew to row forward and ignore his cries, no matter how much he begged. He prepared himself to face what most men couldn't.

And that, to me, is parenting in a single metaphor.

We know what's coming, don't we?

The morning chaos. The meltdown over the wrong socks. The refusal to brush teeth, or buckle up, or just sit still for five seconds. We know how fast things can spiral, how small triggers can become massive storms. We know that logic won't always land, that patience will be tested, and that sometimes—no matter how well we planned—it still falls apart.

But the question is: do we tie ourselves to the mast?

Do we prepare for the storm while things are still calm?

Do we set the tone in advance? Do we rehearse our responses, ready our breath, remind ourselves that their outburst is not a reflection of our failure—but a call for our presence?

Because peace isn't the absence of noise.

It's the presence of discipline in the middle of it.

It's the choice to anchor ourselves—to something stronger than the moment. Our values. Our love. Our self-awareness. The mast isn't there to restrain us. It's there to remind us who we said we'd be when the waters were still.

There are things in life that test us—moments where adversity feels like it's winning. Where every parenting book feels useless, and every so-called "specialist" tip has already backfired so many times that your child now sees it coming. He knows what I'm trying to do… and he's having none of it.

One day, in the middle of a public meltdown at the park—a full-body, screaming, overloaded kind of moment—I found myself frozen. Embarrassed, frustrated, overwhelmed. And then, out of nowhere, something from an old audiobook floated into my mind. Marcus Aurelius. I'd listened to him at the gym, never thinking it would come back in a moment like this. *"Accept what you cannot control. Focus only on what you can."*

So I stepped back. I breathed. And I scanned the scene not as a parent trying to fix everything, but as someone trying to find *his part* in it. What could I actually control right now? My reaction. The environment. The noise. The crowd. The music playing from the car. So I removed the source of overstimulation, calmly and quietly, without force or panic.

And something happened—something simple, but profound. He saw me *take control of the situation* without trying to control him. And slowly… he settled.
That moment changed something in me. It reminded me that I'm not here to control *him*, I'm here to guide *me*. And in doing so, I give him something solid to anchor to.

Reflective Thought:

Parenting isn't about mastering every storm—it's about learning to anchor yourself within one.
You won't always have the perfect response. You won't always be calm. But the more often you tie yourself to that inner mast, the more your child will feel your steadiness when they need it most.

You don't need to have all the answers. You just need to be the one who stays grounded when the winds rise.

A Thought to Carry With You:

"Peace isn't found in the absence of chaos—it's found in your ability to remain calm within it." The Philosophical Dad

Reflective Question:

When the storm begins, what can you actually control? And what are you trying to carry that was never yours in the first place?

Letter 3: The Power of Perspective – What the Stoics Teach Us

There's a story about the Stoic philosopher Epictetus.
One of his own students once stole a small oil lamp from his room. A petty theft. When asked if he was upset, Epictetus simply said: *"He stole a lamp. That's all. I wasn't harmed unless I believed I was."*

He wasn't naïve. He knew he'd been wronged. But his point was deeper:
It's not the event that defines your peace—it's your perception of it.

And when you're raising kids—especially kids with sensory sensitivities, emotional triggers, or just a whole lot of big feelings—you learn quickly that perspective might be the only thing *you* have full control over.

Because the truth is, some days just feel like a barrage of setbacks.
You ask for shoes to be put on for the fifth time. You try to guide your child through a meltdown that seems to last an eternity. You walk into the room and see the baby has poured an entire cup of milk on the couch. Again.

And it's so easy to say, *"Why is this happening to me?"*
But what if it's not happening *to* you?
What if it's just happening?
And what if your power lies not in stopping the storm—but in seeing it through a different lens?

Perspective is such a powerful tool. It can completely shift how we experience a moment. What looks like chaos through one lens might look like growth through another. What feels like failure today might, with a bit of distance, reveal itself as a turning point. And sometimes, two people can live the exact same moment and walk away with entirely different stories.

When you're raising a neurodivergent child, it's so easy to dwell on the hard parts. The therapies, the social challenges, the daily routines that feel like uphill climbs. And when you're exhausted, it's even easier to fall into the loop of *why me?*—to only see what your child *can't* do yet, and miss all the quiet miracles they're doing every single day.

But I've learned this: the more I focus on the things going wrong, the more wrong things I seem to find. And the more I look for beauty—the laughter, the still moments, the unexpected wins—the more they show up for me. It's not about pretending everything is fine. It's about choosing what to give my energy to.

Because the truth is, our children are amazing. Unbelievably unique and full of wonder. We just have to learn how to show them how amazing they are… in a language they understand. And sometimes, that starts with seeing them clearly—without the fog of our own frustration.

Reflective Thought:

You don't need to control everything. You don't even need to understand everything. But if you can shift your lens—just slightly—you'll begin to see your child not as a challenge to be solved, but as a person unfolding in their own beautiful, complicated way.

And the more you see them with grace... the more they'll start to see themselves that way too.

A Thought to Carry With You:

"You don't need a different life. You may just need a different lens."
– The Philosophical Dad

Reflective Question:

What's one moment from today that felt difficult... and how would it look through your child's eyes?

Letter 4: Presence Over Perfection

There's a Greek myth that tells of Hercules standing at a fork in the road.

Two women appeared before him—one radiant, soft-spoken, promising a life of pleasure and ease… the other, cloaked in dust and scars, promising a life of hardship, sacrifice, and real purpose. Hercules, without fanfare, chose the harder road. The road of Virtue.

Parenting often feels like that same choice—daily, sometimes hourly.

Do we choose perfection, appearance, and control? Or do we choose presence, patience, and connection?

One is shiny. The other is soul work.

The world around us doesn't make this choice easy. Social media shows curated lives. Extended family offers unsolicited advice. We carry the expectations of past generations, our own insecurities, and the quiet fear that if we're not doing it all right, we're doing it all wrong.

But the truth is, trying to be perfect—for your child, your partner, your parents, or the judgmental eyes of strangers—is a game you can never win. And worse, it's a game your children don't need you to play.

They don't need a flawless parent. They need *you*.

They need the version of you who sits on the floor and listens. Who apologizes when they lose their temper. Who gets it wrong, and comes back again anyway. Who breaks the generational mold not by being perfect, but by being *present*.

Messy. Honest. Trying-your-best *you*.

That's the parent they'll remember—not the one who made every meal perfect, but the one who knelt beside them in their lowest moment, and stayed.

I remember one morning last year dropping my son off at prep. From the moment we got in the car, he didn't want to go—I could see it in his face, feel it in the air. But I was determined. Determined to be the one in control. To show him, to show myself, that I knew what I was doing. That I had it all together.

The meltdown started on the way and only grew worse when we arrived. We stood in the school playground—parents everywhere, staring. My son crying, screaming, and refusing to move. I looked to the teachers for help, but they just watched. I was pleading with my eyes, but no one stepped in. And still, I pushed. I kept trying to make it work, trying to prove I could hold it together.

Eventually, we left. Exhausted. He settled down in the car. I didn't. I sat there, quietly shattered—not because he'd screamed, but because I'd failed to see him. I'd made the morning about me. About looking like a composed, competent father instead of being a safe, present one. My pursuit of perfection hadn't helped him. It had only made both of us feel worse.

Looking back now, I realize: the moments where I drop the mask and actually *see* my son for who he is—those are the ones that matter. Not the ones where I "get it right." Just the ones where I stay.

Reflective Thought:

Perfection demands performance. Presence just asks you to be there.

Our children won't remember the days we held it all together.
They'll remember the days we knelt beside them when things were falling apart.
They'll remember the steady voice, the deep breath, the way we made them feel seen—even in their hardest moments.

You don't need to be flawless. You just need to be reachable.
That's what they'll carry with them.

A Thought to Carry With You:

"Your presence will be remembered longer than your perfection ever could." The Philosophical Dad

Reflective Question:

Where are you holding yourself to a standard your child never asked for? And what might happen if you let it go?

Letter 5: Anger, Guilt, and Emotional Control

Seneca called anger the most destructive force in human nature—not because it's loud, but because it's blinding. He said it could reduce the strongest men to ash. Not from the outside in—but from the inside out.

I used to think that anger was a weakness. That if I felt it, I'd failed.

But I've learned that anger is not the enemy—unmanaged anger is.
And guilt? Guilt is its shadow. It clings to us in the aftermath. It tells us we're unfit. It plays the worst moments on loop. And it rarely tells the whole truth.

If you've ever snapped at your child, slammed the door, or raised your voice and then sat in silence afterward with your head in your hands… you already know what this letter is about.

You know the weight that follows.

The way your breath shortens when you hear their tiny footsteps behind the door after an argument. The shame that burns when you see fear in their eyes—not because they're afraid of *you*, but because they don't understand what just happened. Because they weren't the cause—they were the witness.

And I know that moment. I've lived it. The guilt that follows is not always productive—but it is a signal. A call to come back to ourselves.

This letter isn't about how to be perfect.
 It's about how to be real, and still choose to repair.

To take the breath next time instead of the bait.
To walk back into the room and say, "That wasn't okay—but I love you, and I'm here now."
To model what it looks like to own your emotions, instead of being owned by them.

Because our children are learning from us—not how to be flawless, but how to be forgiving, and how to come back from the moments that fracture trust.

We can be that example.

It took me a long time to realize that anger isn't the enemy. It's one of the most natural instincts we have. It's protective. It's primal. It's powerful. The real danger is when we haven't learned how to carry it. When we speak from it before it's ready to be heard.

For years, I didn't know how to hold it. If a morning didn't go to plan—if the chaos of parenting, work, and sleepless nights piled up—I'd sometimes snap. at my kids. At my staff. And afterward, the guilt would come crashing in. It wasn't their fault. It was mine. My son, especially, didn't have control over how his nervous system was reacting… *I did.* And I failed to show him what to do with that.

There's an old quote that comes to mind: *"In the morning we carry the world; by noon we stoop beneath it; by evening it crushes us."* That was me. And in my frustration, I used to bring that weight into the room with me—into his space. Into his struggle. I added to his storm when, what he needed… was a steady hand.

Now I see it differently. He doesn't need me to join his dysregulation. He needs to know that *even in his worst moments*, there's still one person who won't abandon him emotionally. And when he's overwhelmed, I want him to know this:

>You don't have to lean into the storm.
>You can lean into me.

Reflective Thought:

Anger doesn't make you a bad parent.
But refusing to learn from it… that's where the harm lives.

There's a quiet kind of strength in emotional control—not the strength to suppress, but the strength to pause. To breathe. To speak gently even when everything in you wants to roar. Because our children don't need us to be saints—they need us to be safe. And when we mess it up, they need us to show them how to own it, repair it, and keep walking forward.

That's not weakness. That's leadership.

A Thought to Carry With You:

*"You don't have to join their chaos
to lead them through it."
-- The Philosophical Dad*

Reflective Question:

What does your anger usually ask you to protect—and how can you honour that without hurting those around you?

Letter 6: This Is the Hardest Job You'll Ever Love

Kahlil Gibran once wrote that our children are not our children.
They come through us—but they belong not to us.

And that truth has a way of breaking your heart wide open.

Because parenting isn't just about raising them—it's about letting go of *you*.
Your schedule. Your sleep. Your expectations.
Sometimes even your sense of self.

And still, we show up.

Over and over again.
Tired. Unshowered. Underappreciated. Unsure.
And somehow, still believing it's worth it.

There's a quiet ache to this job.
Not because it's joyless—but because the joy costs so much.

Because the beauty is often buried inside the mess.
The laughter echoes through rooms still cluttered with toys and yesterday's dishes.
The magic of connection shows up just after the meltdown.
The kiss goodnight follows the thousandth test of your patience.

The moments that melt your heart arrive when you've almost got nothing left to give.

And no one really prepares you for that.

No one tells you that the thing that will undo you the most is love in its purest, most demanding form. Not romantic love. Not fleeting love. But the kind of love that asks you to become someone you never thought you could be—because someone small needs you to be that person.

This job won't give you awards.
There are no promotions.
No sick days. No applause.

Our lives as parents rarely follow the same path. Some of us are raising neurodivergent children, some aren't—but all of us are tired. Some of us in the same way. Some in ways that can't be spoken. Some of us are waiting for someone to reach down and help us out of the hole. And some of us… are that hand reaching down.

We spend our days in motion. Driving from place to place. Planning activity after activity to stretch their minds, calm their hearts, help them make sense of the world around them. It's relentless. It's exhausting. And most days, it goes unnoticed. But we do it anyway—because we believe in who they can become.

That's the thing about this job: it's built on faith. On love that doesn't ask for recognition. We pour out everything we are in the hope that they'll grow up carrying the best parts of us forward—and leaving behind what didn't serve them.

My hope is simple: that my sons and daughter take the lessons I've fought to learn and build on them. That they take my flaws and turn them into strengths. That they carry forward not my perfection—but my effort. And that one day, their children will do the same for them.

Reflective Thought:

This isn't an easy job. It was never meant to be.
It pulls at your time, your patience, your sense of control—and sometimes, it feels like it's pulling at your sanity too.

But you keep going.

Not because you're trying to be a hero... but because you are the hand your children reach for when the world gets too loud. And the truth is, they may not thank you today. They might not even understand the weight of what you carry. But one day... they'll feel it. And they'll remember.

Not the perfection. The presence. The effort. The love.

And that will be enough.

A Thought to Carry With You:

"You're not just raising children—you're raising someone else's parent."
– The Philosophical Dad

Reflective Question:

What parts of yourself do you hope your children carry forward? And which parts do you hope they transform into something better?

Letter 7: You're Doing Better Than You Think

We live in a world that keeps score.

How many hours you worked.
How many dishes are left in the sink?
How many meltdowns happened today?
How many times you raised your voice.
How many things you didn't get done.

And when we keep track like that… it's easy to feel like we're coming up short.
Like we're failing in small, invisible ways that no one sees—but we carry.

But I want to remind you of something that too many people forget to say:

If you're reading this, you're trying.
If you're tired but still showing up, you're doing better than you think.
If you've apologized after raising your voice…
If you've held your child through a storm…
If you've stayed up too late worrying whether you handled it right…
You're already the kind of parent your child needs.

Because our kids don't remember the to-do lists.
They don't measure our worth in loads of washing

or meal variety.
They remember how we made them feel—especially when the world around them felt hard.

They remember that you came back after a mistake.
That you stayed in the room when they pushed you away.
That you whispered, "I love you," even when the day didn't feel loving.

You won't get a report card for this.
No boss is going to pat you on the back and say, "You held space for big emotions like a champion."
No one will hand you a medal for sitting in silence with a child who doesn't have the words yet.

But those are the moments that matter most.

So if you're here—reading this, tired, overwhelmed, maybe wondering if you're doing any of this right—hear me clearly:

You are.
You are doing better than you think.
And your child is lucky to have you.

The hardest lesson I've learned on this parenting journey—no matter which of my children I'm speaking of—is this: nothing works all the time.

You can think you've nailed it. Found the routine. The perfect tone. The magical technique. And then suddenly… it doesn't work anymore. And if you listen carefully enough in the stillness of the night, you might just hear God giggle in the background.

Because no system is perfect. No advice is absolute. Things can feel amazing—until they don't. Until everything changes again.

And that's where your strength as a parent truly shows. Not in control—but in adaptability. In humility. In your willingness to keep learning.

Learn from the mistakes. From the little wins. From these letters. From your own instincts.
Show your child what it looks like to evolve. To self-discipline. To regulate. To lead—not just with instruction—but with example.

Because the world won't wait for them to catch up. It's your job to get them ready for it.

So show up. Be patient. Be virtuous.
But above all… be present.

Reflective Thought:

You're not failing.
You're growing.

You're not behind.
You're building something no one else can see from the outside.

Parenting isn't a test you pass. It's a life you live—one lesson, one breakdown, one breakthrough at a time. Some days you'll feel like you've got it. Others, like you're barely holding it together. But if you keep showing up with love, with intention, with effort… that is success.

You don't need a perfect system.
You don't need a flawless track record.
You just need to keep choosing to be here.

Every time you rise after a hard day,
every time you offer presence instead of performance,
you are becoming the kind of parent your children will remember.

A Thought to Carry With You:

"You don't need to do more. You just need to see what you're already doing."
– The Philosophical dad

Reflective Question:

What truth from this book do you want to carry into tomorrow—and what old expectation are you ready to lay down?

Letter 8: The Weight of Comparison

In ancient myth, there was a boy named Narcissus, so taken by the reflection of himself in still water that he couldn't look away. He wasted away at the edge of the pool, staring at something that could never love him back.

Comparison can do that too. Not because we love ourselves too much—but because we forget to love our own life enough.
We fixate on the curated, the polished, the filtered stories of others—and we lose ourselves in someone else's reflection.

There's a strange kind of heaviness that creeps in through the cracks of quiet moments.

It's not the tantrum.
Not the sleepless night.
Not even the chaos of trying to do ten things at once while your child melts down in the background.

It's the moment afterward—when you sit down, open your phone, and scroll past someone else's perfection.

The smiling kid eating their vegetables.
The spotless house.
The family holiday.

The caption that says "just a normal day," but feels like it's doing more than your best day ever.

Comparison isn't loud.
It doesn't shout at you.
It just whispers: *"You're not doing enough."*
And if you're tired enough, raw enough, that whisper feels like truth.

But here's the thing: it isn't.

Those filtered moments you see? They're *fragments*. Not full lives.
Not full stories.
Not the part where the dad snapped, or the mum cried in the pantry, or the kid threw a toy and said "I hate you" that morning.

You are comparing your full, messy, *sacred* life…
to someone's highlight reel.

And even then, you're still showing up.
Still wiping tears.
Still reading this book because *you care enough to wonder if you're doing this right.*

You are.

You're doing more than the algorithm will ever give you credit for.
And your child doesn't need a curated version of you.
They just need you. Right now. As you are.

The truth is, I do social media too.
I post. I scroll. I try to be present while also building something meaningful.
But even when you understand the game, the weight of comparison is a heavy burden to bear.

And it's not just online, is it?

It's the side-eyes at morning drop-off while your child melts down in the car park.
It's the quiet judgment in the supermarket when your kid is screaming beneath a clothing rack.
It's the subtle glances, the passive sighs, the feeling that you're being *watched*—measured—while simply trying to help your child through their moment.

But here's what I've learned:

Comparing yourself to the expectations of people who couldn't last five minutes in your shoes?
That's madness.

Maybe they'll mention you to a friend that evening.
Maybe they'll say something like, *"That dad can't even control his own kid."*
And maybe—for a second—you'll believe them.

But after that?
They'll never think of you again.
So why should you give more than a second thought to people who don't know your story?

The answer is: **you shouldn't.**

You should give your energy to the rest of your day—your children, your work, your next moment of peace.
And when that quiet moment comes—maybe late at night, or in the car after a long day—**reflect**.
Ask yourself what happened, what went right, what went wrong.
How you reacted, and what that moment may have looked like *through your child's eyes*.

And then, ask yourself:
What can I alter tomorrow?

That's where your power is.
Not in the opinions of strangers.
But in your ability to choose *growth over guilt*.

Reflective Thought:

"Don't waste your time on jealousy. Sometimes you're ahead, sometimes you're behind. The race is long—and in the end, it's only with yourself."
— Mary Schmich

Thought to Carry With You:

You are not failing.
You are doing life.
And that's not always meant to look
good—it's meant to mean something.

Reflective Question:

Whose voice matters more today—the stranger's, or my child's?

Letter 9: Let Them Be Small

In Greek myth, Demeter—the goddess of harvest—loses her daughter Persephone to the underworld for part of each year. And in her grief, she lets the earth go barren.

There's a quiet lesson there: the ache of letting go is part of loving deeply.
As our children grow, little parts of them disappear into seasons we can't hold onto.
But the beauty isn't just in what we lose—it's in what we were lucky enough to hold for a time.

There's this pressure in parenting—unspoken, but constant—to always be moving forward.
To have milestones met.
To have your child be *resilient, independent, ahead of the curve*.

We rush to toilet train, to get them reading early, to have them "well-behaved" in public, and to prove (mostly to ourselves) that we're doing it right.

But in all that rushing… we forget the sacred truth:

Because what we see as delay, frustration, or mess—might just be *exactly* where they're meant to be.
The meltdown over the wrong spoon.
The refusal to put on shoes.
The endless questions, the regressions, the clinging when you need space.

These aren't failures.
They're childhood, in its rawest, most human form.

Sometimes they don't need redirection or discipline.
They need space.
They need your lap.
They need a few more months of baby talk.
They need one more night sleeping beside you.

They need to be small.

The world will teach them to grow up.

It'll teach them to armor up, to filter themselves, to do what's expected.
But you, as their parent—you're the one place where they can be little and *loved for it*.

Let them be soft.
Let them be slow.
Let them be behind, if behind is where their soul is still learning.

Because one day, you'll look back and realize that the moments where it felt like you weren't getting

anywhere…
were actually the moments that mattered the most.

One thing I'm constantly reminding myself is this:
He will only be this age once.

At some point, the rocks he brings home from school "just for me" will stop.
The dinosaur sounds in the backyard will fade.
The made-up songs he sings in the car will be replaced with silence or headphones.
And that thought—it *breaks my heart*.
But it's also the most natural part of life.

My son struggles to talk.
He struggles to express emotion in ways that feel clear to the rest of us.
Both of those things—he's getting better at. Slowly. Miraculously.

But oh, how sometimes I wish he'd hurry up.
And it's not because I want him to be like the other children.
It's not comparison driving that ache.

It's because I want to know what the hell he's giggling at at 9:30 at night while we sit quietly in the lounge room.
I want to understand how he can recreate entire movie scenes with his toys—word for word—without ever having said those words in conversation.

I want to be part of the magic that's clearly alive in his mind.

Mostly... I just want to talk to my son.

But for now, he is small.
And I will let him be.

Because this age—this moment—is fleeting.
And every rock, every dinosaur roar, every made-up song... is a piece of him reaching out in his own way.

And maybe, just maybe, that's his way of speaking to me all along.

Reflective Thought:

"If a child is to keep alive his inborn sense of wonder... he needs the companionship of at least one adult who can share it."
— Rachel Carson

Thought to Carry With You:

Let them cling.
Let them wobble.
Let them grow in their own time.

Reflective Question:

Am I guiding my child forward—or just trying to hurry them there?

Letter 10: You Are the Anchor

In *The Odyssey*, Odysseus doesn't just face monsters.
He faces the sea.
And the sea is relentless—shifting, crashing, pulling in every direction.
But the ship doesn't fight the storm with sails.
It steadies itself with an anchor.

That's you.

You are not the wind.
You are not the solution to the chaos.
You are not meant to steer through every meltdown, predict every mood, or correct every misstep.

You are the anchor.

nd an anchor isn't loud.
It doesn't shout commands or offer advice.
It doesn't need to be perfect.
It just *holds*.

It holds when the screaming starts.
It holds when your child throws words at you they don't even understand.
It holds when your partner is overwhelmed, when the guilt seeps in, when you feel like you've failed.

It holds because someone has to.
And it might as well be you.

Not because you're stronger.
Not because you never break.
But because you know that presence beats performance every time.

Your child doesn't need you to have the right words.
They don't need you to always stay calm or say the perfect thing.
They just need to know:

"When I'm falling apart... my parent doesn't drift."

The truth is, you won't always fix it.
But you'll be there.
And sometimes, that's all they needed to begin healing.

There is a center point.
A place of stillness, where—for just a moment—the world stops spinning.

The breeze touches your skin.
The sun warms your shoulders.
The weight of the day lifts just enough for you to feel the humidity in the air, the rise and fall of breath, the shape of your child as they soften into your arms.

This is what I call the still point.

It doesn't come with advice.
It doesn't come with correction, anger, or even solutions.
It's simply *presence*.
The place your child needs you to find when their world is collapsing.
Because when they can't regulate, when the chaos is too loud for their body to hold—they need your stillness to anchor them.

And I'll be honest with you…

There have been so many times when I couldn't find that point.
When my own mental health, exhaustion, or overwhelm got in the way.
And in those moments, when I watched my son spin further out while I lost my grip, the guilt was unbearable.

Because I knew—deeply—that I hadn't given him what he needed most:
Me. Present. Anchored. Calm.

But here's what I've come to understand…

There's no singular answer.
No clean map to this journey.
Because each of us walks a path no one else can fully see.

And so, I would never pretend to have *your* answers.

This book was never about fixing your parenting.
It was about reaching across the fog and saying:

"You're not alone out here."

Reflective Thought:

"A ship is safe in harbor, but that's not what ships are built for."
— John A. Shedd

Thought to Carry With You:

You don't have to hold everything together.
Just hold your ground.
The storm will pass—but you are still here.

Reflective Question

In moments of chaos, am I trying to control the waves—or simply hold the line for my child?

Final Thought to Carry With You

"Children are not a distraction from more important work. They are the most important work."
— C.S. Lewis

This journey is not about perfection.
It's about presence, grace, and the quiet courage to keep showing up.

There will be no awards for this work.
But your child will carry your love into every room they walk into,
long after the toys are packed away and the house falls quiet.

So take a breath.

You've done more than you think.
You've loved harder than you realize.
And that love will echo, even on the days you doubt it.

This letter may be over—but your story isn't.
And neither is theirs.

Keep showing up.

About The Author

Phillip Deam is an osteopath, educator, and father of three, but above all else, he is a man who shows up—even when he's tired. After years of studying human movement, pain, and recovery in his clinical work, he found his greatest test—and greatest growth—within the walls of his own home.

As a father of a neurodivergent child, Phillip's world shifted from theory to reality. What began as quiet reflections late at night—after the kids were asleep and the house had finally settled—slowly became letters, essays, and stories written to himself, and eventually, for others.

Under the name **The Philosophical Dad**, Phillip shares a unique blend of ancient wisdom and modern parenting. His writing is honest, unfiltered, and deeply human—never pretending to have all the answers, but always reaching for something deeper than just advice.

This book is one part journal, one part reminder, and one part quiet conversation with the tired parent who still chooses to love, lead, and begin again tomorrow.

To learn more, follow the journey, or subscribe to future letters:
   www.thephilosophicaldad.co

More From The Author

If this book spoke to something in you—if it found you on a tired night or helped you breathe a little deeper in the chaos—there's more to come.

Phillip Deam, writing as *The Philosophical Dad*, shares monthly reflections, letters, and insights on parenting, philosophy, and showing up with presence—even when it's hard. His writing continues through:

- **Monthly meditations** delivered straight to your inbox

- Other titles in *The Philosophical Dad* series

- A collection of warm, family-focused Christmas books

- Future audiobooks and spoken letters

To stay connected, subscribe to upcoming releases, or join the quiet parent community:

www.thephilosophicaldad.com
Gumroad Store – Subscribe or Explore Other Books *(update this with your live link)*
Instagram: @the_philosophical_dad

You're not alone in this.
You're just human.
And that's more than enough.

Thank you for reading Meditations of a Tired Parent. I hope that if nothing else, it helped you realize that you are not alone in this journey.

I'd like to let you all know that my tiktok account - the_philosphical_dad is always open for messages if you ever have any questions.

The End

www.ingramcontent.com/pod-product-compliance
Lightning Source LLC
Chambersburg PA
CBHW042319090526
44583CB00025BA/3207